KEEP A LAMP OF FAITH

More of Ronnie's Sermon Snippets

MIKE PEARCE

DEDICATION

This book is dedicated to the memory of my father. Also published to help promote his understanding of human nature and help encourage Christian values which are lacking in the world today.

CONTENTS

Acknowledgment
Preview

ACKNOWLEDGMENTS

The author would like to thank Christine Pearce
for reading and checking through the manuscript.

PREVIEW

Church sermons can send some to sleep but the
examples given in this book will help you to reassess
your own values and relationships towards others and
the world toaday through sometimes serious and
sometimes amusing examples . (See also Ronnies
Sermon Snippets.)

1 BUILDINGS

Beauty is a far stronger and greater thing. It is never shallow but demands strength and goodness. Beauty on its own is not enough, unless the thing we build is useful. Our characters are not monuments to be gazed at but buildings to be used.

It appears that when you are going to make something out of stone, you have to consider what part of the country it is going to be in, because climate affects stone. A lot of heat. A lot of frost and a lot of wind will make it wear out quickly. Barnak stone is best in very cold parts of the country, as it is the hardest of the English building limestones. You also must be very careful to see that it is facing the right way, for there is a right and wrong face to expose it to the wind and the rain. If you have the wrong face things will eat into it, or in a sooty place dirt and smuts can cause astonishing damage and it will break into pieces.

The process of building using bricks is like the process of building the building of our lives and each one of us go on building the House of life. Some people never seem to grow up. They build their lives like the baby built his first brick tower, so their lives totter. and they wonder why many make the mistake of thinking that foundations are of little consequence. The importance of a firm foundation non other than Jesus Christ himself to build your life on Him assures you of a foundation strong and secure. Upon that foundation you can build a character, dependable and trustworthy because it is built on solid goodness.

When you leave school. Some of you will go to different parts of this country or to other countries. I cannot tell you what storms you will have to face in your lives. Only that they will come suddenly, so see to your foundations now. Make sure your face will be turned the right way to be able to resist the weather and the storm and so we pray "Use us o' Lord and make us fit to be used.

2 EASTER

Nature and art are here. The flowers from the garden, the music of the choir each contributes to the honour of our risen Lord. The joy of Easter comes from the fact of the living Christ who can enter into all the experience of our life. The call today is for realism. He is the Christ of our common life. The easter message meets the loneliness and purposefulness of this age in which we live. The joy of Easter is the joy of great certainty. Christ has answered the questions- Whence do I come? Why am I here? What is my destiny after death? I come from God. I belong to God. I go back to God. Goodness is stronger than evil. Easter is full of hope. Life is stronger than death'

Michael Faraday was coming to the end of his life and a friend came to his bedside and asked. What are your speculations?"

Faraday replied in astonishment, "Speculations? I have none. I know whom I have believed. I rest my soul on certainties."

We need to rest our souls on certainties- the empty tomb- the risen Christ.

At the entrance to a cemetery was written 'Fuerunt'- meaning they have been faithful always. Over the gate of a churchyard, it said 'I am the resurrection and the life. To the unbeliever, the dead are but memories. To those with faith the dead are living, working, praying friends whom nothing but the dullness of sense hides from sight.' Jesus said 'because I live, you too will live and by that faith and in hope the Christian is content to live and to die.

3 MESSIAH

Before the last war in Germany hate events reached their climax. A man who was a Christian at one of the meetings could not stand it any longer. "Christ is the Messiah," he shouted. Nothing happened, except a few people turned around and looked at him with surprise at the intrusion. Another spoke out more clearly. "Christ is the only Lord and Leader." He was lynched. The Nazis understood those words – 'Leader'. The second man did nothing more than the first, except interpret the word Messiah. The word Messiah disappeared in a vacuum.

4 THE BODY OF CHRIST

St Paul give us a picture of the church as a body with all its different parts important in themselves. They know their use and perform it to the advantage of the whole body. Christ is no longer in this world as a body. If he wants a task done for Him within the world, He has to find someone to do it. If He wants a child taught, He finds a teacher. If He wants to sick person to be cured, He finds a physician or surgeon or a nurse. Literally men and women have to be the body of Christ in the world. Today one of the best ways of testing the efficiency of a school, or a church is to find how much its members care for one another. St Paul says, 'rejoice with those that rejoice and weep with those that weep.'

5 STARTING WITH THE RIGHT KIND OF SHOES

We depend on each other. We keep to ourselves is a damming indictment. All around u families live with great sorrows, great tragedies, great deprivations. The loneliness of and sense of uselessness of some elderly people and thousands of mentally sick and yet so many people say we keep to ourselves. A few years ago. On a very large poster which used to help sell a certain brand of shoes, two happy children could be seen starting off on a very long walk. The children were making a good start for they were wearing the right kind of shoes. We must all start right. Shoes for example go in pairs, left and right and are very little use separated. We are often partners with those around us. We are helped to make fine progress along life's road. It is only on a cross that a man can die with outstretched hands. But by that sign we are saved, and we must live.

6 WHO ARE YOU? WHAT ARE YOU MADE OF?

Those of you who have read Alice's Adventures in Wonderland will recall the conversation between Alice and the caterpillar asking contemptuously, "Who are you?"

A recent television program showed how scientists had shown that the body has a lot of different clocks, not just one. One might have 40-year-old heart, 60-year-old kidneys and a thirty-year-old brain. Scientists say that it might be possible to extend life by slowing down biological clocks. A diet of fish plays a vital role in brain function providing a chemical that helps electrical connections to work efficiently, in other words make the sparks fly.

Who are you? Are we treating the body like a machine? Who are you? Much of the same question was asked centuries before. Psalm 8 tells us of a man who went out of his tent one night and looked up into the sky. He had no idea of the immensity of the universe as we have, but he thought it was very big. As he looked up into the night sky, he asked, "What is man that you O God take any notice of him.so. What is man or woman?"

Some years ago, they published what a man is worth. 5 shillings they said and with inflation an extra 75p. So much calcium, iron and a few gallons of water with enough phosphorus to make a box of matches. It was not very impressive; a chicken would cost more. But the fact does not add up to the truth. Would you go on to say your wrong? A man is a two-legged creature with no feathers. O is he a gorilla. For centuries men have tried to define what they are. A man is one who cooks meals, laughs his head off when highly amused and the only creature who says his prayers.

One could say they write sublime books such as the bible, Shakespeare Pilgrim's Progress, beautiful poetry. All of which which will endure as long as men can think and read at all. Men also peddle atrocious rubbish and cheap clothes in frowsy little shops and stalls. They are loving and kind and uphold the laws of the land, but they can be lazy, cruel and neglectful, ill-treating children.

They have brilliant skills, alleviating pain by discoveries or they are the only creatures to discover and manufacture poisons so deadly that a small amount could kill of the population of the whole world.

Men may build cathedrals, breathtaking in their immense and exquisite beauty. They may build soaring bridges, fine factories, much better than the dingy horrors of the past. They may design weapons of mass destruction to smash to a million fragments those cathedrals and homes and all within them.

So, is man just a bundle of chemicals? No, he isn't. This doesn't scratch the surface of the truth

We need an interpreter. Without one, we would say he is a mixed-up creature, clever and stupid with the cancer of evil embedded in his very nature. Jesus said, "Men were capable of rising to the full height of their true real manhood if they knew who they were, and he called them the ('Children of God')".

Are we not answerable to God for the way we treat

nature? Taking everything, poisoning rivers and seas. Are we not answerable for our relationship to others in private and public life? Each of us is responsible for the character we make in the few years we have on this planet. After all the only thing we shall take with us is the character that is forged and worked out in the light of the answer to the God who made us. This is the Christian answer to what is man. He is the one who because of Jesus can dare to lift up his head in hope.

Think about it. When we look around us today, we see that we are passing into an age of lawlessness. Everybody wishes to do as he pleases in the long run. However, lawlessness makes life impossible. Mankind did not take many steps in the direction of civilization without discovering even at a tribal stage that tribal laws were essential. If tribes were to survive, sooner or later every nation, every individual, has to make the choice, not whether we will live by any rules at all, but which set of rules will he choose. What we ask for today is for a recognition of the law of Christ, the law of love between men and God and men and women.

7 DECAYING FAITH

Tennis cannot be played without a clear aim or purpose in mind. St Paul said 'So run, that you may. attain'. The worst attitude in life is to drift without an aim in life. Boredom could well be described as a psychological wasting disease. There is a link between faith and having an aim or purpose in life. Those who do not believe in anything, often do not strive for anything. Today decaying faith has gone hand in hand with increased boredom. Too many people do not know what they want from life because they do not believe in anything in life, let alone the life hereafter. We need to ask to see a faith in the hearts and minds of people in order to combat meaningless and the resulting boredom and presence of which life holds up.

Everyone who plays a game knows he must play to win. A purpose or aims likewise is essential for the whole act of living. Involvement is important. Not just watch. No one can get the feel of a running track unless he has actually run a race on it. He knows the battle of the mind and the battle on the feet. To understand what life is about a man must live it to appreciate what faith is about. A man must exercise it. What we ask for is not to be a grandstand critic of Christian faith but to be involved performers running in the race says the New Testament. Run patiently. That is like the long-distance runner, running with an eye on Jesus Christ the lead runner and perfector of our faith It is not that Christianity has been tried and found wanting. By many it has not been even tried.

8 SUFFERING AND PAIN

Somewhere at this very moment a family are sitting broken hearted. Their son was brought home yesterday, killed by a road accident or drowned in a river canal or the sea. Hundreds of homes are passing through some dark valley of sorrow at this very moment. That's not all right. Now thousands of people, children, teenagers and older folk are suffering pain of one kind or the other. Elsewhere other people, good people are suffering from an incurable disease There are many disasters, famines and tragedies in this world.

Why, why does it happen? is the inevitable question asked by so many people. Why does God allow it? Christians claim God is a God of love so why does he allow all this suffering pain and war. His question of suffering is one of the greatest tumbling to faith

One needs to consider an immense amount of suffering is caused directly by men's own stupidity, selfishness and negligence. The neglect of known risks is very common, often through cost saving or just laziness. Even traffic accidents are simply caused sometimes by people who imagine they can drink to excess, or drive vehicles or lorries with known faults, such as faulty brakes. There are also neglectful parents, the distress and heartbreak after crimes, savings stolen, victims savagely beaten-up and man's inhumanity to man.

We have seen the suffering and miseries caused by war, seas of blood and horizons of fire. Also, biological warfare, nerve gas, and other agents, as well as nuclear threats.

Millions if not billions of pounds are spent on the means of curing further tragedies .in a world desperately short of housing, schools, hospitals, doctors, nurses and scientists. Nations squander wealth on armaments to defend themselves against a war which each dreads.

To confuse acts of God with acts of men is thoughtless, misleading and utterly irresponsible, for it leads people away from the truth instead of towards it.

Suppose builders on a building site said, 'blow the plans and the blueprint everyman for himself, lets workout our own ideas.' When you saw the finished house, you would say, "You tell me there's a designer or architect behind all this. Don't make me laugh." What proportion of all the people in the world do you suppose are following a designer's blueprint? A pretty small number. Many of course don't know about it, and many don't want to know about it. They prefer their own ideas. If the result is pretty chaotic, can you blame the designer

God sends no pain or suffering to anyone. Let us not look upon someone stricken with disease and say this is the will of God. Or when a small child drowns in an undercurrent say, 'Thy will be done'. This is sheer blasphemy. What kind of father would design a tumour of the brain? On a morning when the newspapers announce yet another disease is conquered and banished, let us then say, 'Thy will be done'.

The intentions of God for the world are good and loving. However, man may strive to overcome that good with his own evil.

We started with the question why? and have not got very far in answering it because it is a question no one can answer. We may have thrown a little light on the subject. Christians do not know why men suffer but they do know with glorious certainty is how to come through victorious over suffering. The Christian believes in a God who protects his children, not from death, any more than he did for his own son. But in death and through death there is a glorious faith, we all can find.

9 A MORAL SOCIETY

A tradition involves carrying a portreeve around the town hall after the Civic Sunday. This ceremony is called the 'beating of the bounds' or 'common walk'. At each stopping point (halting) a boy who accompanies them is turned upside down on his head and asked to give a name of the place he is in. If he fails, a constable gives him three of the best with is truncheon and in this way the name is impressed on the boy's memory for all future occasions. All this dates back to 1320.

In Kipling's second Jungle Book you may remember how the jungle beasts slyly encroached upon a large Indian village which was too occupied with its own comfort to realise what was happening. Slowly these enemies crept forward to destroy crops, slay domesticated animals and drive the inhabitants away one by one until a once thriving village was part of the jungle again. Here is perhaps a parable for our own time. We live in a society the root trouble of which is the confusion of moral distinctions. We call it the 'permissive society' the harvest of this can be seen daily in our newspapers. Integrity is the most precious commodity in British public life. John the Baptist preached 'make straight the way of the lord'. He called for men and women to think straight and live straight. To be men and women of integrity. St Peter was nicknamed 'the rock', reliable, unshakeable in a storm and courageous. To stand alone. Martyrdom is the willingness to stand for what is right in life.

God said to Abel, "Where is thy brother?" What would we reply if God asked us that question? Where are those who are different from us, less fortunate than us, and more desperate than us? Do we make a place for them in our lives? Are we concerned for them?

A radio drama told of the events leading up to the hanging of a convicted criminal. The plot centred on five hanging ropes in addition to the one prepared for the criminal.

One rope was for his parents, who had denied him the right to be loved.

The second was for the school authorities, who saw him as a problem never as a human being

The third was for a politician who had feared to vote on a bill which would have wiped out the slums which nurtured him.

Then fourth was reserved for representatives of television whose programmers had made crime and immorality more attractive.

The fifth was for the average citizen of an average community whose indifference and apathy had made all the rest possible.

"Where is Cain? thy brother?." The time calls for men and women to live a life of maximum service in an hour of need. An appreciation for those who give time, energy and talent to serving others often at a cost to themselves.

10 KEEP A LAMP OF FAITH

The decision of faith is to fight in the small corner of the battlefield, where man finds himself and by faith to be a light in the darkness.

Paulinus was a man who lived in the fourth century and who came to the conclusion that his civilisation was crashing to destruction. He decided the only thing he could do was to keep alight a lamp in a particular shrine and that's what he did. It seems to me what each of us can do is keep a lamp of faith in the midst of surrounding darkness in answer to the ill-omened materialistic view of life. The lamp showed to the people that opposite is true.

On a dark night by the seaside, we sometimes see the water glow with a soft light. Every wave has a fringe of flame. It is called phosphorescence. It comes from tiny sea creatures floating in water. How do they shine? They have no light in themselves. They cannot make light, but they can absorb it. All day long they soak themselves in the light of the sun, then at night when the water is troubled, they give it out again.

God is our source of light, the nearer we get to Him the more light we shall absorb and the more light we will be able to give out in the darkness. An Old Testament prophet of 6th century BC said "You know well enough man what is good. For what the Lord requires from you to be is just to love mercy and to walk humbly with your God"

11 WHAT DO WE MISS LIKE THE POTTER?

Jeremiah 18 /2 "Arise and go down to the potter's house." He was told to go down by God and tell the people what he saw. He saw five things, four of which he mentions

Firstly, a heap of broken earth, a mound of soft shapeless clay with a handy pan of water. This was the raw material.

Secondly, he saw the wheel with a treadle. To make it move, this was the power and the energy.

Thirdly he watched the potter's shaping hand as it moulded the soft clay into shape. This was the mind that lay behind things.

Fourthly he saw the finished article for the home. This was the end product, the justification for the whole process.

Fifthly, he intentionally misses. He failed to see the furnace where the vessels were heated and baked. This was the cleansing fire of discipline by which the soft clay was made hard and durable.

What would you see in Shakespeare's words 'There are sermons in stones?'. But some people only see the stones. It is often with a beautiful, finished vessel or bowl, a piece of choice art, some people only see the clay.

In the world today there are many beautiful things made by the devising mind of the master potter God. But there are people, some of them very clever and learned, some scientists, some philosophers, some poets and in all the wonders of the world and of human life they see only clay.

The clay is there. They are right. We are linked to the natural world in which we live, but is it enough to explain it, is all just clay? If you debate man's destiny, the here and the hereafter, they answer clay that is all they see. Some see the wheel there is no doubt about the wheel. We all know it is there, but some never see beyond it. They look at life and the world and see it only as a whirring, ceaseless, senseless round of things.

It is right to admit the wheel. You can trace it in day

and night, in the exact recurring of the seasons, in the rise and fall of civilisations. The world is grass that lives and dies and lives again, but is that all? To see the wheel is good. To see only the wheel is as much ruin as it is folly. The man who sees the wheel without the potter, God himself, who is the eternal explanation, is as much of a fool as he who sees the clay without the living spirit that gives it breath.

Some are fortunate to see the potter's hand. This is good, but again is it enough? They see some dim purpose that masters things, but they do not know anything further, if deeper. Most people who have sorrow find God, but they often lose God as the father. This is because they deny the kindness of the hand because it hurt. There can be no meaning, no hope, no peace in a God who is not a father. It is in the face of Jesus Christ that we see God's face. In Christ's love and mercy and forgiveness we know there's divinity that shapes our ends.

Jeremiah saw the finished article. He picked it up. Look at this. What do you think of it? It was once clay, then one day the potter picked it up, he put it on the wheel, he moulded and modelled it, slapped it and caressed it there.

But he failed to see the fire. If he had, he would not have been falsly dubbed today 'the weeping prophet' The iron in him would have been purified into steel. But like all sensitive souls the thought of fire hurt. We love this fire how it is gentle and confined when we can put our hands to it and warm ourselves. But when we have to go through it in difficulties or perhaps pain and suffering, then it is when we ask in rebellion, why we find life with its challenges overshadows us to throw us onto God that in us he may rise to overcome it. It is in this that we see. We see the world as a vale of soul making.

12 POISON IN OUR SYSTEM

There was once a man who had three nasty boils and he went to the doctor and asked for each of the boils to be treated and removed. The doctor said, "My dear fellow, I can do nothing permanent with these boils unless we get rid of the poison in your system which is causing them." So too the human race is very sick and having many more than three boils in the social and moral order wants to be rid of them. But this human race does not grasp that the trouble is a poison in its system and the sickness is that of a deep derangement in the relation of mankind to the creator. God is shaping his vessels here and now and the one thing he wants is character, tried, purified, refined and tested. Men and women who display in their lives eternal values, things that cannot be bought with a price, are the things that matter. They are not reported in the press. You become a saint, where God puts you by living your life whatever it is, to the glory of God. In the end it is worth its cost for our own sake and Christ's. This is the goal and meaning of our own existence.

13 PEACE

What is peace? It is not just the absence of war. It's certainly not the imposition of the will of a person or group on another person or group. The Old Testament word is 'shalom' and that can be translated as the 'fulness of life or the sharing of God's gifts'. So, peace can be brought about by the finding and sharing of all that God has to give. Only then is there peace.

14 SUB-THINK

Here is an eye opener. 'Sub think' is where images are flashed on a cinema screen every now and then. Nobody consciously remembered them, but they bought the items advertised. Thousands of people were being unconsciously influenced to behave in a certain way. The deadliest thing about it was of course that it was unconscious. People didn't know they were being influenced. There is a great deal of 'sub think' going on right now in our society through advertising making it increasingly difficult to get back to standards on which morality is built. It can result in vandalism nationwide, moral cancer imperiling the lives of innocent people and resulting sometimes in horrifying brutality. This calls for leadership especially for the youth today.

15 TAKING THE RISK YOURSELF

The bible tells of David when the Philistines held Bethlehem and how he wished for a drink of water from the well at Bethlehem. Three of his most loyal followers fought through the Philistines and drew water from the well and brought it back for David. But what did David do? He took the water and poured it on the ground saying, "Far be it from me that I should, this, is this not this the blood of men that went in danger of their lives."

You see the true leader will never be willing to profit by the risks of others. He must take the risk for himself, and to take the responsibility for other people is always a serious thing. The number of those who are willing to take responsibility is somehow decreasing, and the number of those who are too ready to say that somebody ought to do something about things is increasing. We need leaders who will influence the whole tone and nature of society and quietly hold up, like the pillars of some foundation, the true and lasting values by which the majority wish to live. There are no dropouts from a meaningful life. Progress has never come by sitting down and waiting for the other fellow to begin. Progress has never come by sitting around talking about it. It has come when men have caught a vison and taken off their coats and rolled up their sleeves to turn that vison into reality. Such leadership and vision you will say needs strength and moral courage.

16 CUTTING THE THREADS OF FAITH

The curse of our modern life is man's decision that God does not matter, that man can manage on his own, that man is the maker of all things. An old Danish fable tells how a spider slid down a single filament of web from the lofty timbers of a barn. There he spread his web, caught flies, grew sleek and prospered. One day he looked up and saw the thread that stretched up into the dark unseen above him and thought how useless it was. He snapped it but his web collapsed and soon it was trodden underfoot. The truth is that when we try to do without God we also collapse when we cut the thread that holds us in living touch with the unseen above us. We fall.

17 THE RIGHT ANCHOR

A wise old sea going pilot was talking about anchors. It was his opinion that in spite of their later design and increase of weight, modern anchors do not hold ships against the press of weather as well as the old familiar kind that had the cross bar at the top. The modern anchor, he complained, plays sudden tricks. It loses its grip when you need it most or turn over and drags whereas the old kind went straight down and stayed held by its cross. "Mister," he said, "It's like that with life," and he was right. It's the old kind of anchor. We need the kind that goes straight down and gets a firm grip on eternal truths and abiding realities.

18 A SPIRITUAL TONIC

From time to time, when feeling a little low, most of us take a tonic, a pick me up, to help us on our way. These are physical tonics. But there are other forms of tonics, the mental and spiritual ones. A holiday, a visit to the seaside, or the pace of the countryside with scenes of natural beauty. Magnificent music or art, fine choirs and orchestras, uplifting church worship. Relaxation through books, poetry and films, even fishing help ease the stress of modern living.

There is too also the spiritual tonic we get from hymns. They stimulate minds and penetrate consciences in them. We find varieties of religious experiences. These are a spiritual tonic for me. I set aside a time to remember. Someone has said that memory is the power to gather roses in the winter and what a wealth of roses there are. They bring colour and warmth to the damp and desolate atmosphere around us. I recall some of those men and women I knew long since and lost awhile. Those for me who inspired affection, loyalty and love and then the real meaning of this somewhat hazy text, 'Blessed are the pure in heart,' shifts into focus and purity of heart has a familiar face or faces.

Many of these people were unknown and unsung. Obscurity and hiddenness was the lot of most. Full many a flower is born to blush unseen. Yet flowers like this are vital parts of the beauty of the earth. These hidden men and women whose lives unknown make up the beauty of the world. They were not perfect Transparently good they may have been, but they were aware of their own faults.

This purity of heart was never obvious to them, for purity of heart is like humility. Thinking that you've got it is a sign that you haven't, but others saw it in them. They affected the world through their lives and personality, rather than through words. They were ordinary people whose lives were extraordinary, for they showed a special quality. These people were content, happy to serve where they found themselves, among their own people and cast light on the daily lives of their family friends and acquaintances. Those with strong and noble characters set us the example in a world and age where obedience is little thought of.

Where every man does that which is in his own eyes and authority counts for little.

These are the people Jesus describes as accounted worthy to attain that world. Remembering them, we find encouragement and strength for our own living, for if we have faith in the possibility of the victory over hate, purity over lust, the victory of charity over greed, the victory of unselfishness over self-seeking, the victory of humility over pride, we can rise above all that wants to drag us down and submerge us. We live risen lives already. Then we can discover a depth of meaning and wonder and a hope the world cannot give.

We see then it is a moral need to remember and a moral need to be grateful for these people.

19 LIGHT IN OUR DARKNESS

As I looked back through the ages, I saw men always returning to this image of light holding torches, setting candles in shrines, lighting their way and one another's faces

Light was at the beginning of creation; it began the whole story. 'Let there be light' It is the favourite image of the New Testament of Jesus' mission to give light to those that sit in darkness. It is the highest duty of those who follow Him, to let their light shine before men.

'In thy light shall we see light,' so the psalmist and Bunyan's Pilgrim was told. Not just to look for the light and for the shining city set on a hill that was his destination. But to keep the light in his eye so that when he lost his way and stumbled, the light stayed with him.

20 GOOD GIFTS AROUND US

There is no life that is independent. No life is private. Harvest reminds us of the fact of our complete dependence in life upon the services of other people and how we are bound up together in the bundle of life. Every one members, one of another. If we have received God's love, it involves us in the obligation to share that with others. There is enough food in the world for man's need but not for man's greed. This fact, that we are members one of another, should influence our treatment of other people in the community in which we live.

The fish was a sign used by early Christians when they met together to avoid torture and persecution. In Oxford in one community all elderly people were encouraged to keep a black cardboard fish in their houses, so that in times of need they could hang the fish in their windows. Milkmen, postmen and neighbours were asked to keep a sharp lookout so that help could be brought to anyone displaying this distress signal. You see love will always involve us with people, peril and pain.

Dependance on each other means caring for each other. This is the first message of harvest. The second is something we are always in danger of forgetting -our dependance on God. Have you ever thanked God for the wonderful gift of your eyesight? We take these good gifts for granted. We only value them when we lose them.

Do you remember the parable of the ten lepers? It is a mirror of mankind. You see one man returning to render thanks. One man? Were there not ten cleansed, but where are the nine? The facts are that 90% gave no thanksgiving. What happened to the others? Why did not they all come back? Why was there no word of thanks upon their lips? Where are the nine? Oh Lord, I had to take the dog out. O Lord I was up late the night before. Were there not ten cleansed, one returned giving his thanks. Will that be you? Only you can tell.

21 TO SERVE

To get on in the rat race it is necessary to trample on other people. Ruthlessness and determination takes priority over consideration, neighbourliness and concern for other people's welfare. They will come to see the meaning of being members, one of another and that the words 'no man is an island unto himself' were never truer than they are today. Their job then will be undertaken in love of God and their neighbour, it is the essence of God's love to give, rather than grab. We are told that the son of man came to serve rather than be served. To lose our vision of God when we are at work, is to be blind to our maker in a major area of our life here on earth

22 PRIDE IN CRAFTSMANSHIP

Sir Angus Watson talked to a drystone wall builder. They came to a wall, and he said, "I built that wall and if it is not interfered with it will last for 300 years." He admired the excellent craftsmanship and tried to estimate how long it had taken to build. He asked the man, "What profit have you made from the work?" The man was silent for a few moments and then replied, "I suppose that by the time I had finished the wall, which took me nigh on thirty years to complete, I was better off by about three pounds."

Asked "Don't you feel sore that that you made so little from so great a labour?"

"No," replied the man. "You see I built that wall."

23 DAY OF REMEBRANCE

The historian can only tell you the outward framework which make up events which caused what it felt like. A lot of people here today have memories of people they knew and love. Into my mind comes the young university graduate, Jonny, who joined the fleet air arm. He helped to defend Malta. He was shot down into the sea and spent two days in a rubber dingy in the Mediterranean. He went on flying too long hours, too many air scraps, not a break, not a rest, because Malta had hardly anyone left who could fly a plane and very few planes were undamaged. Finally, he was relieved only to be killed in an air crash a month later. Such a person would be hard to forget if he died in bed. Because he died that way, he was unforgettable.

There was also a quick little rugby scrum half called Paul. He was small of stature but sturdy. No little man by his stature as a character. Good company, because so trustworthy. When Germany broke the French front in May 1940, the tanks reached the English Channel near the mouth of the Somme and moved northward along the coast towards Calais. They wanted to cut off the British army from its retreat to Dunkirk. Somebody must at all costs stop them. There was hardly anyone around so the commanders rounded up any one they could find, miscellaneous oddities and sent them into Calais. Paul was killed in Calais. They couldn't hold out for long. Four tremendous days, just long enough, only just, but not long enough to let the British army cover those vital miles nearer to Dunkirk. The history of the wars says this: by their discipline, courage and stout-hearted endurance, they enriched the history of the British army.

We have a duty to remember at this distance of time. Our feeling is not of sadness but of gratitude. To give thanks for heroism, self-sacrifice and victory is not to glorify war. The sense of right would be poorer without such a remembering. Each name on the roll of honour is the name of someone who is someone who lives on in the sight of God. Our worship this morning tells of a faith in the living God who calls us to live with Him in eternity. They tell of God's guarantee that this is so in the life of a man called Jesus who was done cruelly to death but of whom it was said only three days later, 'He is not here, He is risen'. Through faith and trust in this same Jesus we share the resurrection of life.

Death is swallowed up in victory on Remembrance Day. God goes out to a dangerous world where evil is at work nourishing mindless brutality. War should find no place on humanity's agenda. For the future man possesses the power to obliterate himself, or he can choose life in partnership with God the father of all. More and more people are waking up to the realization that this crucial decision stares us in the face here and now. The future is in the hands of young people and the fostering of friendship is the way to understanding and reconciliation. Our best tribute to those who fought and died is to work hard to give this vision substance in the family, in school, at work and among our friends. Pray God then for a better ordering of the world in the ways of His kingdom of love and peace.

24 VOCATION CALLING

How seldom do we find this word in people's minds or on their lips today? How often do we hear what's the pay? the wage? the salary? the working hours? the pension at the end? and seldom now what's the opportunity for helping? With how little vision do we consider the work we are called upon to do in this world. The calling of the shepherd can be every bit as much a vocation as the calling of a doctor. To all of you, can there be a vocation greater than leadership? But in leadership there can be continual new risks. The risk of being built up into a publicity personality. The risk of so magnifying our own office that we magnify ourselves. This leads to an assumption of superiority, but superiority not leadership as in our lives we meet people of importance, power, ability and perhaps even genius.

Yet we may be aware that they lacked greatness because they lacked humility. One senses humility in the man who attaches more importance to the work he is doing than to himself and is not anxious about his status or reputation. He does others the courtesy of cooperation and is ever ready to give credit for the help he receives from them as he takes them along with him in his vision and his venturing. What the Bible says is often uncomfortable. If a man is desirous of being one of the 'top people'- he must aim at becoming one of the bottom people. If he desires to be a master, he must become a servant and sacrifice will be inevitable and perhaps costly. That is what leadership means.

25 REALITY IN OUR SURROUNDINGS

We must also meet the sorrow the pain and disappointments and difficulties in the lives of others. All around us today human families live with great sorrows, great tragedies and deprivations. One chief concern is the enormous rise in crime which calls for a need to tackle social deprivation which can encourage criminal tendencies, bad housing, overcrowding, unemployment, inadequate leisure facilities and broken homes.

Government, both local and other need to bring to their work those qualities of responsibility, devotion and unselfishness on which the efficient discharge of their duty rests.

The bishop of Coventry was visiting a school near Delhi and asked to see the chapel. There was a small wooden cross hanging on a thin wire and behind it there was no wall. He looked beyond and there was a washing line, people with brushes sweeping the path and cattle and sheep. "For heaven's sake how can one pray in such a place?" he said. The man behind said, "We want you to pray with your eyes wide open, that's what we do in this place. How can we worship God without looking right through and seeing people and seeing the rugged reality of things?"

We need to see them, so that we can lift them up before the throne of grace. To pray with your eyes wide open that is the purpose for us all. God needs us in life. Situations in the guise of our neighbour in need. 'If you have seen your brother then you have seen God' is not a slick phrase I have thought up but the words of a 4th century Saint. This is where God is real in the heart of human struggle. Sharing our neighbours' suffering takes us right to the heart of the gospel After all isn't this what the cross was all about?

26 FOUNDATIONS

Foundations are important as well as change, continuity as well as personal effort. The personal unselfishness, the personal love of what is true and excellent. These are the individual offerings a school needs.

The brick by Michael Quoist--The bricklayer laid a brick then with a precise stroke of the trowel spread another layer and without a by-your-leave laid on another brick. The foundations grew visibly. The building rose strong, and tall to shelter men.

I thought Lord of that brick buried in the darkness at the base of the big building. No one sees it, but it accomplishes its task, and the other bricks need it. Lord what a difference. If I am on the roof top or in the foundations of your building as long as I stand faithfully at the right place. We must remember those who in times past have laboured for the good of this school. With this memorial his body is buried in peace but his name lives for generations to come.

27 OPINION POLLS

Imagine three men go up in a balloon a doctor, farmer and a clergyman. After a while they have difficulties with the ballast. One has to be put out over the side. Who would you put out first? I am not going to embarrass you by asking your answer. I can already see he clergy man's cassock acting as a parachute.

Let us take it a step further. The farmer represents food, the doctor health, the clergyman-religion.

Now who would you put out first? Again, I am not going to ask for you answer. I have used this to emphasise the word irrelevant -having nothing to do with. For thousands of people today, religion has nothing to do with their lives. The curse of modern life is man's decision that God does not matter. That man can manage. That man is the master of all things.

There are many reasons for this attitude but one of the main ones is the great advance in science and technology. Things have changed greatly from 100 years ago. Imagine a lady in a bonnet and bustle picking up a glossy magazine. Imagine the astonishment, even terror of seeing cars hurtling along a motorway and the ear shattering noise of a jet aircraft making height. And what about television in everybody's room?

Much has changed in this school. An old gentleman who returned to the school for the laying of the foundation stone told me he was going to go round the school to see if there were any changes. But has life changed so much? Cloud and sunshine, health and sickness, life and death, pleasure and pain. These are the basic facts of life. They only change the colour of their clothes.

28 WHAT DO WE BELIEVE IN?

So, let us ask the question, is the Christian faith outmoded as some try to tell us it is? The answer is no. We cannot make such statements on any kind of showing. People are the same, life is basically the same and their needs stand out as ever they did. What are their needs?

People need, as we all need, something in which to believe. This is half the trouble today. No one believes in anything or in anybody anymore. The trouble in Britain today is that we no longer believe, no longer trust, and when a people no longer believes in anything the quality of its life drops down.

We need a firm basis for living a foothold across the swamps of life on which to set our feet. What does the bible say about this? In the beginning the heavens declare the glory of God, the earth is the Lord's the fullness thereof. The sea is his and he made it. The bible sees the world with God at its centre. It teaches us too that this is a God who cares. What a difference that makes. Somewhere at the heart of all our experience of life there is a living, loving God. Though I walk through the valley of the shadow of death, I will fear no evil, for thou art with me.

Ann Sedgwick, a great novelist and invalid, was confined to bed for years. Her bones were so brittle that if she moved, they broke. She could say in spite of this, life is a great struggle, but life is beautiful to me. There is a joy in knowing I lie in the hands of God. She had mastered life. She was strong. Her secret lay in the psalm's words, 'Blessed is the man whose strength is in thee.'

So many today say life is meaningless. They never stop to ask the questions. Where do we come from? Why are we here? and what gives us our destiny? God in Jesus Christ gives us the answer. I come from God, I belong to God, I go back to God. What simpler philosophy of life could you have than that? It delivers us from the nightmare of meaninglessness and gives us something to live for.

29 THE SIMPLE HERITAGE OF TRUTH

When people point to the chaos of present-day life, where is God in all this? The answer is just here in these very consequences of the violation of His laws, where violence and strife follow on suspicion and greed. Where unhappiness follows selfishness there is thy God. After all the waning of the word crisis is judgement.

There is a great danger today that we are content to live off the spiritual and moral capital of the past without putting in much of our own new spiritual investment. This will never do, for if we are indebted to the past, we must have responsibility for the future. This applies in many walks of life. If we are grateful for our inheritance from the past, let us see to it that we cultivate our own faith, hope and responsibility that these things are entrusted to us to hand down to the generations yet to come. But there is all the difference between the veneer of tradition and the solid base of human heritage of truth which never changes. God forbid that we should give up that heritage of our fathers.

30 JUBILEE

Let the trumpets blow loud and long throughout the land. What a happy year it will be, for it is the year of the jubilee. These words were written nearly 3000 years ago and are taken from the book of Leviticus. In the Old Testament times the Jews used a ram's horn, hollowed out and polished as a trumpet. It made an odd, deep hollow sort of sound which carried along the valleys to the hills on the other side. It was a traditional way of calling the attention of the people to some special happening.

The Hebrew word for a ram's horn is yobel. The 'year of the yobel' is the year of the trumpet or jubilee. This was kept after 50 years, and they had a sort of national year off. Our silver jubilee is half that and as we look back over those 25 years of the queen's reign, we are grateful for an example of service untiringly done and of duty faithfully performed. The queen has stood for the continuity of precious values for national dedication moral duty and religious faith.

31 CHANGE AND SERVICE

Many years ago, I remember reciting with all the members of the class the prophet 'Pistle Water Boy' whose name they were proud of. Yes, much changes. But time will not allow further reminiscences. The prophesy of the old magician Merlin of King Arthur's court. Kidwelly was Carmarthen, but Laugharne will be the greatest of the three. Certainly, some will see in recent years a fulfilment of this prophesy and Laugharne is no longer just a dot on a map. But there has been change in the town itself. Many of the old landmarks and schoolboy haunts are missing. Orchard Park, a new housing estate, a new school in Will Johns field, elderly people's bungalows.

A complete transformation of Frog Street and a lot of Gosport Street and the Grist. Tommy Rowland's woodshed (the old pistle) by the corporation gave the name to the members of the local rugger team. Pistle Water Boys is a name they were proud of. Yes, much change but time will not allow further reminiscences.

Here in this ancient and much-loved church of St

Martins, men and women have laboured over the years to lay the foundations of Christian faith. Just beneath me here was Miss Cunningham. Up there on the organ was Williams and in Sunday school was his father Mr Maurice Williams and others. Still today there are those who give their time and energy and talent in the instruction and guidance of the young people of this town. The whole structure of society will change possibly beyond recognition, but there will be an increase in wisdom as well as knowledge for the two are by no means the same.

Changing towns, changing buildings, changing fashions. Even changing modes of shopping can only give us satisfaction if under our feet is a firm foundation. Foundations matter. Watch any good team of builders at work in this or any other town and note what care goes into the basic structure. It is useless building on shallow or shifting foundations. That way lies disaster. Long patient, skilled work must be put down in the depths before even a brick or stone can be seen above the ground given that we need not fear whatever the strains and stresses put on the building.

We must be grateful too for the men and women who have built on these foundations and have stood for and kept before us the continuity of those lasting values and traditions which are ours today. Such continuity of loyal service is a most essential requirement in all departments of life today but especially in education.

32 WE ALL HAVE A PART TO PLAY

In the last few weeks, we have witnessed a community feeling that most adults have forgotten ever existed. There has been a deep sense of unity up and down the country. Some dismal jimmies claim it will be short lived but nevertheless they cannot deny that it is there.

When you go to a theatre the curtain goes up and the scene is set. It might be a farmhouse, a castle, or a cave and when there is another scene you find yourself looking at something altogether different. People have been busy often in a great rush to change things round and get them right for the actors to perform. At the end of the play all the actors come on and we clap and sometimes cheer them, but we never see the scene shifters like that. Yet the play could hardly go on if the scenery wasn't there, so in everything there are people behind the scenes. It is a case of working together. Everyone is doing their part. St Paul puts this well in the parable of the body - having gifts that differ according to the grace given to us. Let us use them.

33 WHAT MAKES YOU WHAT YOU ARE?

Have you ever suffered from backache? If you have you know that it can be rather grim. You get little sympathy from your friends. Even the doctor will tell you you can't do much about it as some people have backs and others haven't. Faced with a situation like this you will do anything to get rid of the pain. During the holidays I found myself in this position and in the search for a remedy. I picked up a book with the title, 'Total fitness in 30 mins a week.' As I browsed through it, I read before you set out on a fitness programme you must ask yourself who you are. If you want to be a tennis player or professional footballer or a skier, you need a higher level of fitness than an ordinary person so the programmes should be different.

As I read further, I came upon the next question- What makes you what you are? Some people say it's the signs of the zodiac under which you are born that controls and affects our lives, so each day and year they are guided by their horoscopes. Mine yesterday, which was my birthday, read, 'This year will bring steady uptrend in your material circumstances. It's a year of exciting events which will change the pattern of your life'. Does it literally make sense to believe everything is fixed in the stars and that everything that happens to us is fixed by fate or destiny? If so, we are not responsible for our actions, and it follows from this that Adolf Hitler should not be blamed for what he did, and that Albert Schweitzer should not be praised for his lifetime spent in providing medical care in West Africa. Both these had no choice it was their destiny. The foolishness of arguing such cases as these soon becomes obvious. If our choices are not fixed by fate, the stars or destiny, what factors do influence our lives making us the people we are?

Some will say it's hereditary. What we look like, our inborn aptitudes and abilities. A boy may be musical because his father or mother was musical. He may show ability in drama, maths, or science again because of this

Some will say environment plays a major part, including your surroundings and how you are brought up. You may be well fed and nourished as a child leading to good health in later life. Alternatively, you may be neglected, undernourished as a child leading to poor health and lack of confidence. In spite of hereditary and environmental effects, many actions in our life are influenced by choice. We choose food, clothes, friends, interests, manner of life, career, to be married or remain single. We all have choices that help to shape the kind of life we lead. A major choice will provide the general direction of a person's life but sometimes freedom to choose will be lost.

There is the fable of some pigmies who bound up a giant. They were much smaller than he and their thickest ropes were like pieces of thread to him. He let them bind him around a few times knowing that whenever he liked he could snap their flimsy ropes. He thought it would be amusing to let them go on. Suddenly to his horror he found they had bound him around so many times he could not break free at all. We can lose our freedom of choice by becoming bound to the same habit. Again, drifting through life appearing to make no real choices, is in itself choice. Drifters have chosen to opt out of responsibility. They resent discipline, neglect to train for anything and for a while appear to be having a good time. Ultimately their freedom is seriously impaired because opportunities to lead a more purposeful life slip by and cannot be recovered. Eventually their moral and mental powers atrophy -become useless.

The great composer Schumann was a great pianist, but he was not satisfied with the performance of his weakest finger, the fourth one on his right hand. In order to strengthen it he fastened it in a strained position and then practiced with the other fingers. When the time came to release it he found to his horror that the finger was useless and his whole right hand was badly crippled. It governs what we believe about the world about human life and about the goal to which we are moving.

There is one great choice in life which determine how all other choice are made Everyone has to make a choices between acknowledging God or disregarding Him

Our values and belief in God is not just agreeing to the

fact that He exists. It affects our whole way of life, the standard values by which we live, qualities like honesty, truthfulness, reliability. Somebody said that the world as we live in it is like a shop window in which some mischievous person has got in overnight and shifted the price labels around so that the cheap things have the highest price labels on them, and the really precious things are priced low. We let ourselves be taken in.

To be a Christian means choosing a life in which serving others matters more than being served, in which love matters more than greed, in which life is given to God and for others rather than lived in a spirit of selfish acquisition.

34 HOW DO YOU REGARD YOUR WORK?

What is your aim in life going to be? To have a good time? Be successful in your career? Win the lottery? Become famous? Or help people try to make the world a better place, lead a decent life.? When St Paul's Cathedral was being built Sir Christopher Wren took a walk around the building talking to some workmen.

Carpenter- "What are you doing?"

 "I'm chipping this piece of wood." He said as if this job was hated most in all the world

Mason- "What are you doing?"

"I'm earning a living." It was felt that if he was left a pile of money he would never have worked again.

Man sweeping up dust and chippings- "What are you doing?"

"I'm helping Sir Christopher Wren build this cathedral."

Will you regard your work as a way you get money or as sharing in God's whole purpose for the world?

35 AND EZRA STOOD UPON A PULPIT OF WOOD

It does seem there is a growing desire amongst people to gain knowledge of their past. A development which may be associated with their quest for a future. About 400 BC the Jews returned to their own country after captivity in Babylon. Nehemiah, their leader was engaged in rebuilding the city of Jerusalem. He had a meeting with the head of the people to find out what was the size of the problem. Meanwhile Ezra, a lawyer, had been sent by the king to restore the neglected law in Jerusalem. He was to read the book of the law to all the people.

As they listened memories flooded back of the former glory of their nation. Their present plight, surrounded by rebuilding reorganization made them despondent and their courage changed from little to less. Nehemiah joined Ezra on his wooden pulpit and called to the people. "This is the day holy unto the lord. Mourn not, nor weep. Neither be grieved, for the joy of the Lord is your strength." The people went away joyfully as the law would guide and encourage them.

On one occasion an Oxford professor, F.H. Bardley, had a puncture in his back tyre of his bicycle. An undergraduate saw the professor prop his bike against a wall and then attach a pump to the front tyre. "I say sir," he exclaimed. "You are pumping up the wrong tyre. It's the back one that is punctured." "Indeed," replied the professor, "but surely they communicate."

We are fortunate that there is no such uncertainty of communication between this town and the school and that this happy and welcome link has gone on for many years. What better message can we here have to help with problems of rebuilding and reorganization. What better message could you take away with you, than that from Nehemiah.

36 DEALING WITH DOUBT AND UNCERTAINTY

I am a little tired of the dark loving crepe hangers. These people who criticize, deride, knock and do nothing themselves. Those who constantly look on the black side and who tempt us to drown our sorrows in the sterile stagnation of dismal despondency. We know there is a cause for anxiety in the world today but there always has been and always will be.

Which newspaper recently wrote religion is dead, morals are slack, family life is breaking up, social injustice is rife, the worship of God is a pastime for fools and the elderly? It was not a newspaper but written around 2,500 years ago before Christ by a near contemporary of Ezra named Malachi who was describing the condition of his day. What may you ask are the grounds for optimism?

I must tell you of one of your own roadmen. The bishop was walking through Wolverhampton a few days ago and stopped to chat with a roadman about unseasonable weather. The roadman prophesied that it would rain continuously for 70 days' "Oh surely not," said the bishop. Why the rain that caused the flood was only forty days."

"Maybe," replied the road man but our drains are much better than they were in those days."

These times call for men and women to live a life of maximum service in an hour of maximum need. A large number of people are doing this, not least among these, some of our young people. Sometimes we can't see the results of our striving. Sometimes our devotion to principle leads to division. Sometimes we have to bear the burden of doubt and uncertainty in what we are doing. Sometimes this can lead to mental and emotional turmoil. But where we find people prepared to accept this, we can be certain that God is at work creating justice, honesty, compassion and love. This is the very heart of Christian experience. People can hear you preaching without knowing it.

37 SINCERITY-"BY THEIR FRUITS YE SHALL KNOW THEM"

The picture is about a stonemason in classical times or maybe a sculptor. The chisel slips and the smooth surface is spoiled. Fortunately, there is no one to see. The worker fills the hole with wax. The client cannot see the fault not till the sun shines hot and the wax melts.

The genuine job is without wax with no flaw to hide.

Sincere, is the word. Sincere without wax, with no false show. A genuine article through and through. The bible's word is goodness. A good man is good throughout. Wherever you meet him you will always discover soundness. It is what Jesus had in mind when he said, 'by their fruits ye shall know them.'

The mayor of Wolverhampton in 1855 was a bit of a poet. In his first year of office, he likened it to a ship on its outward-bound annual voyage. At the end of his period of office he wrote, "We piped all hands-on deck, and giving each man a dream of comfort from a bottle of hope, bid them cast their fears and differences to the wind."

Handing over his duties he said, "Sir, this noble vessel is committed to your command. I wish you a safe and pleasant voyage and to see her in peaceful security with satisfaction to the owner and crew. So, as you leave today, we wish you and your crew a safe and pleasant voyage and may the joy of the Lord be your strength."

38 PENTECOST

The disciples experienced resurrection with the same difficulty. They simply failed to adjust themselves to the situation. They doubted, they feared. They didn't know what to believe. Their outlook on life was imperfect. Their idea of the spiritual life was found wanting. They had a mental revolution in themselves. It was only at Pentecost that the last shadows were dispelled from their world. Then, only then, did they grasp the whole of this revelation in all its truths and made it part of themselves.

The resurrection is more than a glorious event in the future. It is an experience in the present. Now this is a triumph over death, for which we do not need to wait until the graves are opened. This new life is going from darkness to light, from prison to freedom, from death to life. St Paul said, "I die daily." He saw that the love of sacrifice had become part of his experience, no longer clinging to the life of self which has no resurrection.

The cross is a means to an end. It finds its explanation in an empty tomb. It is an entrance into life. Not a mode of death. It is from our dead selves then that we must rise to newness of life. The ascent of man begins from the moment he lifts his heart in desire after God. It means a resurrection of the soul and body. It is a conscious living relationship with the father and the son Jesus Christ. The life that is started by God is also sustained and developed by Him.

39 SIN AS A DISEASE OF THE SOUL

The word sin is losing its meaning. It is nor regarded as dark at all these days. We need to realise that sin is not a dirty discreditable thing which smells of the slums and goes about in rags and in fear of the police. Sin is not simply vice, which rots away, the odour reels into the gutter, sin is a disease of the soul, of every soul.

We need a different life, a life with a new power in it and a new footing under it. We need a new centre, not a transformation but transposition. The majority of British people need to be converted to Christianity. The term Christian has become a very useful label. But `terms like fair play, truthfulness, loyalty, the brotherhood of man, these do not belittle Christianity. As St Paul meant it is very obvious that no merely formal routine can help a man much these days. Yet it is the time that there are countless numbers in our own country who are spiritually without the vital experience of Christ which is gloriously offered in the New Testament. Christianity has become for them a form rather than a farce.

40 HOW DO WE KNOW CHRIST IS RISEN?

Dick Sheppard cried out in St Martin in the fields in London, "We are, to put it bluntly, not working enough for Jesus."

"How do you know that Christ is risen?" someone asked a fisherman whose faith in Jesus seemed very simple.

"Do you see those cottages near the cliff?" the fisherman he replied, "Well sometimes, when I am far out at sea, I know that the sun is risen by the reflection in those windows. How do I know that Christ is risen because I see his light reflected from the faces of some of my fellows every day and because I feel the light of his glory in my own life."

Here is a motto for our spiritual life to take back with us into the world on this Easter night. English history is sometimes written as though it were the record of man's battles and rebellions and the births and deaths of kings. But we know that this is not history of our land. This is the history of the common people, who lined their common life in fellowship one with another. There we find the national life flowing steadily on from age to age. So it is with the history of the church. It is the history of devout people who believed in God and handed on the great traditions from age to age. A church may have as its aims, social enjoyment, good singing, good financial backing, but it stands for more than those things. If it stands for anything, it must stand for the power of the living God exercising this power to reform life, to renew character, to change hate to love, selfishness to unselfishness, impurity to purity, unkindness to kindness and revenge for forgiveness.

To culture the life of God in the souls of men is the idea which many people have about the extent to which religion is to influence life. They think that the claims of God are met as part of their life. Some fixed portion of their life is given to religion. They devote an hour or so on a Sunday to church going, a few minutes of hurried prayer in the week, and having done so, they dismiss religion from their thoughts for the rest of the week. But our Christian religion must be all or nothing.

Take my life and let it be consecrated lord to thee. The principle of Christianity is to permeate everything with God.

Ask yourself, is my conscience left tender and enlightened? Have I a stronger belief in the good of life? Has there been a strengthening of will and heart to resist temptations? Has it become easier for me to believe in goodness, truth and righteousness? Do I entertain kinder feelings to my fellow men? In short am I loving as if I am praying? Is the rest of my life in the home, the office, the mill, the shop, kept in harmony with those desires and feelings which I express in church?

41 CREATION

Our bible is full of creation. It begins with a statement about it in the beginning and it ends with a picture of a new creation. In practically all the official creed of the church we make the affirmation 'I believe in God maker of heaven and earth.'

On this Sunday known as 'Creation Sunday' we are faced with such questions as, what this business of life is about? What are we here for? Is there a plan of life about what we are here for? Is there a plan, a purpose? If so, what is it? Where are we? and are we in each scene the actors or the spectators?

42 TIME

Most of us take the passing of time for granted. We give it little or no thought. A plaque on an old clock puts this well -

When I was a child and laughed and wept, time crept

When I was a youth and waxed more bold, time strolled.

When I was a man, time ran

Still as I older grew, time flew

Soon I shall find as I go on, time gone

Is time then the marker?

43 IGNORING THE BEAUTY AROUND US

William Wordsworth wrote

Our birth is but a sleep and a forgetting

The soul that rises with us on our life's star

Hath had elsewhere its setting

And cometh from afar

Not in entire forgetfulness

And not in utter nakedness

But trailing clouds of glory do we come

From God who is our home.

Hence in a season of calm weather

Though island far we be

Our souls have sight of that immortal sea

Which brought us hither.

Can in a moment travel thither

And see the children sport upon the shore

And hear the mighty waters rolling evermore

The Christian faith would be quite impossible if we did not believe in some form or other that the world was made by God to fulfil some pattern and some purpose of his. It is not merely that our actions are to be controlled and understood only by reference to Him. It is also that the very stage on which our little act is to be performed was designed by Him. Not only does He direct the play, we can usually see something of the author in it.

When we study the theatre, we may reasonably hope to see something of the designer. God must somehow be revealed in his universe if it is His at all. It is for man to explore Him in it. For the heavens and not only the Bible declares the glory of God.

One of the dangers of these days is that we very rarely have time to stop and think about our surroundings. We are so obsessed by getting meals and clearing them away, worrying how to provide for the family, doing the household jobs, going to work, tapping the typewriter, satisfying the customer, teaching the class, sitting on the office stool, answering endless letters, mending endless socks, that we forget that pulsating eternal life in which alone we truly live and we fail to hear the waves of that immortal sea that brought us hither.

Why is it that the dawn chorus of the birds makes our whole spirit a throbbing glad response? Why is it that the lines of poetry which we love, repeated to ourselves can take us in imagination right out of our sordid surroundings, so that we find ourselves on a dew drenched highland with the sun shining and the peat oozing, and the lapwings crying and our spirit worshipping our souls. For a moment we have sight of that immortal sea.

In a similar way why is it that not only beauty, but truth, can produce a similar effect which can suddenly stab the mind with a thrill for which there is no language, so that words to which we have assented all our lives are suddenly believed and statements have a significance we never suspected so that we not only know the truth, but feel the truth and our will is challenged to respond to it. It is because truth is part of eternal reality as beauty is.

I read the other day of a woman who was in the kitchen one Sunday morning preparing the Sunday dinner feeling bored. She turned the knob of the radio expecting something quite different from what she heard. Then suddenly a voice expressed something that she knew was part of the eternal truth of God and that Sunday evening she sat down and wrote this to the speaker, "Suddenly you said something that made my life feel very ugly."

The letter went on to say, "I don't suppose I shall have the energy to post this letter, even if I finish it and, in any case, I am sure I shall not have the energy to put things right and alter my way of living. And I don't know why I am writing at all."

She was writing because in that one sentence of truth her soul had sight of that immortal sea. She knew that she belonged to the eternal and lovely and infinitely beautiful things. How often we too could write down the words she used. Suddenly some perspective of the truth can make our lives very ugly.

These gleams of beauty and truth are as through someone we had loved and lost. As if a quiet voice had said, "Don't you remember?" As though in a foreign land, we should hear our own dialect. As though in a concentration camp almost secretly, the hand of a friend should grasp our own. As though after years of loneliness we should receive a letter from our old home.

Goodness has the same effect upon us just as we are moved by beauty and by truth. An example of outstanding goodness and especially of self service moves us to the depths.

44 FINDING SOLACE IN FEAR

And when the fight is fierce,

the warfare long

steels on the ear the distant triumph song

and our hearts are brave again and arms are strong

It is important to realaise that this response to the eternal is part of God's plan for us. How true are the often-quoted words of St Augustine, "Thou hast made us for thyself and our hearts are restless until they find rest in thee."

During the great war one of our soldiers in what was called the forgotten army was fighting his way through the Burmese jungle in what they called the green hell. The steamy climate, the tropical fevers, the poisonous snakes, the buzzing insects by day and the mosquitoes at night. That awful endless tangle of jungle which they had to cut their way through day after day. Their Japanese enemies sometimes high up in the trees sniping at them. It was not surprising that this man began gradually to lose his grip and became exhausted and depressed in body, mind and spirit. Then at last when he was going to give up the mail was delivered and in a letter from his home there were sentences which painted again for him the little village in the Cotswolds in which he belonged. The grey church tower with the elms clustering round it, the rooks stumbling into their nests, the sound of the church bell, the glory and peace of the evening sky

A sense of serenity and deep joy filled his heart and he rose up a different man, though far from home his soul had sight of the place to which he belonged. The place which he had come from and to which he longed to return. These terrible experiences would pass. This exile would end. There was still England and a Cotswold village and his own dear folk.

He was not going to break down and lose his morale or his grip on life. He belonged to England.

As we go on our journey through life it is good to remember that anything that deepens our spiritual sensitiveness and strengthens our sense of real values and makes us rejoice that we belong to God, is worth all the suffering. This may well be the cost in a social set up, planned as ours is.and that things we toil all day to find, like money, fame, popularity and social status have to be given up. Just as at eventide as little children give up their toys when the nurse calls them to bed.

45 DEATH AS A JOURNEY

Death is rather like the modern emigration officer, who deals strictly with the baggage. When we embark for a foreign land, he may say, "You cannot take this, you can only take that." We can take kindness the power to love, the capacity to worship, and the power to serve and to apprehend the truth. So many of the things we wear ourselves out to collect have to be left in the quay when we embark at last in that immortal sea which brought us hither.

46 RADIO NOISE

I want you to imagine that I brought with me in the pulpit a portable wireless set. If I had, I should place it beside me and turn on the knob labelled volume to its full extent. Then I would turn the other knob through a large number of stations quickly and you would hear voices, many of them in different languages coming from every part of the world and speaking on every conceivable subject. Then, if that were possible, I should tune in to a voice talking about religion in quiet steady tones and of how God is love and power purpose.

Isn't that a parable of what is happening today? The volume of sound is immense. The noise of clamorous tongues bombards the ear.

We turn the knob to the station marked 'international' and what a babble of tongues assails us. What disputings and misunderstandings. The sound of war and threats of war are all we hear on the international wavelength.

Let us turn the knob now to the station marked 'political'. The loud booming voice of the threat of communism meets our ears.

We turn the knob to a station called 'science' and we find for many years now men have worked to discover and release energies which could blow humanity to pieces and possibly destroy life on the whole planet. Man, it seems to claim, is the roof and crown of all things.

We turn the knob to the station marked 'religion'. Here the voice is very soft, a still small voice, and it pleads that God is love and power and purpose. This comes to us this evening when we ask Why are we born? What is the business of life about? What are we here for? Is there a plan and purpose for us? If so, what is it? Is there any evidence of such a purpose? Where is there any convincing trace of a plan or a pattern or design? It does not make sense this tangled world. We are not getting anywhere. We are just blundering along victims of fate and choice and accident. All our dreams and hopes and idealisms, and struggles are a mere forlorn futility.

The hospital chaplain leaned gently over the bed of the pathetic little cockney whose attempt at suicide had missed its mark. "Why did you do it Alf?" he asked. Accusation stood strong in Alf's tired eyes, but his voice held only a weak wisp of sound.

"It just wasn't no use going on, there ain't no good news left in the world no more. If there was, people would come running with it." The sin of despair haunted the cockney's hopeless words nevertheless those words probed deep into the hearts of this bewildered and bewildering generation.

Is there any really good news still in today's world? If so, what is the essence of it? Why aren't we better equipped and more eager to come running with it. Few do not go about saying these things of course. Not in so many words, but deep down in the hidden recesses of many a soul some believe there is a radical twist in the very constitution of the universe. Has God a plan? and looking around we feel that the prophet Isaiah might have been writing for tod when he said, "If one looks into the land, behold darkness and sorrow and the light is darkened in the heavens thereof.". Some believe there is a radical twist in the very constitution of the universe which will always defeat man's hopes make havoc of his dreams and bring his pathetic optimism crashing in disaster. Is it your own experience the psalmist advised us when the low mood came to address our own souls and say why art thou cast down O my soul? There are numerous people who know perfectly well that their soul would answer "Cast down how can I help it. Life has been so different from what I hoped, so full of thwarting and frustration and this struggle to achieve something like a decent character, what a weary business that has been. This troublesome self. Ten, twenty years ago I was still fighting that, and I am fighting the same thing still and what's the use. I feel so tragically ineffective and futile. Don't talk to me about the divine purpose in life."

Feelings like this force us up against the most crucial alternative, the most inescapable. The alternatives are despair or faith darkness, futility, ultimate night, or the vision of God standing within the shadow, keeping watch over his own. There is no third way. We should not decide until we have included the fact of Jesus in our evidence and considered His life, death and victory. We know life has a meaning by looking at Jesus' character and God's purpose for all humanity. Our destiny is through the grace of God and the response we make to it, to be raised to the measure of the stature of the fullness of Christ. We know life has a meaning from his cross. We watch Him in our imagination, hanging there, his body tormented, his cause defeated, his soul deserted. If those at the foot of the cross had heard Him cry from anguish and say he was deluded. He was wrong. He hoped in God, trusted him but he does not exist. Or if he does, he is callous, careless and cruel. Go to you homes and forget all I have told you if he had spoken this.

We should have not seen the logic of the situation, yet we listen. We hear a voice coming down through the years with unspeakable assurance and without a quivering note of doubt. "Father into my hands I commend my spirit."

There is a window in a north country church which shows Christ as the light of the world. The main idea is perhaps borrowed from Holmean Hunt's great picture, but it is developed differently. Here the Christ holds the lantern and, in the background, lie some of the great buildings of history. While beneath is depicted some of the sorrows and sins of the world. The murdered, the fighter, the pain stricken and the suffering. Also, mourners are seen with figures with tender faces lowering a coffin into the grave. Amidst all the sins and sorrows often stands the Christ shedding out a steady gleam of light. Life does have a meaning and a purpose and a goal. We come from God. We belong to God. We go to God. We are not poor struggling creatures, the doomed playthings of chance, accident, and futility. We are getting somewhere. We are moving onwards to a day when this suffering, tormented, creation shall see the last of the travails of its soul and this corruptible shall put on incorruption and this mortal shall put on immortality and God shall be all in all.

To see other publications below by the author visit **snappysnappybooks.com or just search Dr Mike Pearce Amazon books.**

Many of these books in these volumes are also published individually

SNAPPY SNAPPY COLLECTIONS:

Volume 1. BUSINESS AND SELF CONFIDENCE

How to be a Successful Business Weed
Clingers, Creepers and Scramblers
How to Deal with Life's Snakes and Ladders
Trust-Nothing but a Must
Know Your Students and Build Your Image
Hidden from the Heart but not Forgotten
More Pens for Pops
Charity Shops

Volume 2. IDENTITIES, HANG UPS AND CONCERNS

I Herring Gull
Pulvi Royal
I am Termite
Go Fat Go
Make up-Revealed
Fertility Stones and Chocolate Eggs
Captain Grottbuster versus the Grey World
The kittiwakes Warning

Wastefulness-Bone and Urine
Tails, Tales
A slice of Slang with a touch of Cockney and a drop
of Dorset
Mr Hamstrings Dinner

Volume 3. HORROR AND HISTORY

The Living Fossils
My Therizinosaurus
Human Termites eat London
Pigeons Splat London
Glass Anemones Tentacle-ize London
Beware of Cucumbers, Apples and Pigs
The Cornish Urchin
Baby Toes
Googolplex of Mice
Screaming Alley
The Night Mare
Queen Rat on Deadman's Island
Dead Donkey Lane
Old Mother Nature laughed and Laughed
The Plaster Room

Volume 4. RELIGION AND HOPEFULNESS

Pattern for Purpose God's and Man's designs
The Littlest Oyster
Tuppeny Hangover
In a Dark, Dark Corner was the Holy Ghost
The Little Shepherd Boy's Gift
Spider in the Tomb

The Sparrows' Last Soul
The Pawnbroker's Souls
The Red Church Doll
The Boy who found Christmas
The Eggstraordinary Easter Egg
Little Mary
Shepherd's Purse
Sitting next to Angels
The White Lily-St Mildred-Patron Saint of Thanet

Volume 5. TIDE AND TIME

The Shell Man
The Shell Lady
The Watcher on the Fal
The Rock Pool
A Call under the Sea
Pocket full of Starfish
The Scrofula Infirmary
Till my Lips were Salt as Brine
The Man with a Book on his Head
Coloured Bricks
The Girl Under the Paeony Tree
Nothing but Leaves
The China Blackbird
The Man who Collected Figures
The Rusty Gate
Time Runs Dry (a play set in a care home)

Volume 6. FAIRY TALES AND POEMS

The Nursery Rhyme Cat
 Cats at Christmas

The Tuppeny Bear
The Giant and the Giraffe Boy
The Giant's Toothpick
The White Cockerel
The Old Pot and the Golden Shoes
Ball Rooms
Exodus to a Leaf
The Forlorn Fruit Fly
Two Sleepy Boys
Mrs Light and Mr Dark
 I'm Just Going to the Bathroom
The Tulip Tree
The Man who always Sprinted
Bits and Bobs (Poems and short stories for children)

Volume 7. A VARIETY OF WOMEN

Photosynthetic Women
Absorbed by a Woman
The Slothful Wife
Betty's Barcodes
Valentines Cards
The Lady loves Red
The Woman who Smelled Books
Boy, Could She Smell!
The Lady who loved Hairspray

Volume 8. CHRISTMAS BOOKS

Impy Christmas
The Little Shepherd Boys Gift
The Boy who found Christmas
Oh, father Christmas what yer going to do?
Nothing but leaves
The Tuppeny hangover
The China Blackbird
The Tuppeny Bear
Cats at Christmas
I Hate Christmas

Volume 9. HIDDEN PERCEPTIONS

Silhouette on the pier
I'm not a dinosaur
Mr Mucus
The golden steps
Napoleonic Frankenstein

Volume 10. MANY CURIOUS STORIES

The house that cries
The paint brush
The man who collected smiles
Jack and the ivy
The stolen baby
The angels quest
The silly isles
Wilderness Way
I am shadow
The lift

Volume11. CHRISTMAS BOOKS 2

Christmas butterfly
The man in the library
City of laughter, city of tears
Blower Armageddon
Happy Christmas
Antman
A fairy journey
The top of the hill
The Christmas visitor
Ring up an angel
The Christmas raindrop

Volume 12.FAITH AND FAME

Fight for Faith (Gordon of Khartoum)
Angel 1818 (James Blundell)
The Saint who carried his head (St. Denis)

Volume 13. A CORNUCOPIA OF SHORT STORIES
The cursing stone
Punch and Judy (New version)
Touch of Kent dialect
One in 20 million
Be a used seed (Finding new horions)
'Open Arse' (The maligned Medlar)
Wings of colour
Elephant pin-cushion

Volume 14 PLANTASTIC
One in twenty million
Be a seed(Finding new horizons)
The open arse (A maligned medlar)

Nothing but leaves
Exodus to a leaf
The tulip tree
Photosynthetic women
Shepherd's purse
 The girl under the paeony tree
Jack and the ivy
Baby toes
Half a flower
How to be a successful business weed
Clingers creepers and scramblers

Volume 15 INSECTASiA
I am termite
Mother of hundreds
The living fossils
Human termites eat London
Brief encounters with insects
Spider in the tomb
The forlorn fruit fly
The Christmas butterfly
Towers of wax
Antman

Volume 16 TA TA TALES
Condiment kiss
Half a flower
Towers of wax
Gee haw whammydiddle
Peeping Tom
Flowers in the snow
One hundred
Life's escalators
Swallowed by a whale

Volume 17 Golden O0jamaflips
Mother loses leaves
Mothers of fertility
A gender fluid tree-The Mulberry
The golden chamber
The golden tongue
The little white stool
The wedding dress
I am white aphid
A letter to Lady Ellhorn
I'm coming for you now
Biscuit man
Left behind

OTHER STAND ALONE PUBLICATIONS at snappysnappybooks.com

Red Fred Cell and Friends (Human Biology - advanced level
Ronnie's Sermon Snippets
Viking Bay-Natural History (Broadstairs, Kent)
The World of Wax
God rest you Merry Scrooge
Napoleonic Frankenstein
Satan's stars
HOP to Heaven
The White Lily-St Mildred-Patron Saint of Thanet
Brexit Rhymes
Earthly Quietus
Could you become a serial killer

ABOUT THE AUTHOR

Dr Mike Pearce is a scientist interested in behaviour. He also was a lecturer in human biology and health at a college in Canterbury, Kent. He has written over 100 short stories as well as a many non-fiction and self-help publications

For more information see snappysnappybooks.com

9 798803 242635